LIVING WITH ADHD

ABDO
Publishing Company

LIVING WITH ADHD

by Tad Kershner

Content Consultant
Elizabeth Hastings, MD, Developmental and Behavioral
Pediatrics Fellow, University of Michigan, Ann Arbor, MI

LIVING WITH HEALTH CHALLENGES

CREDITS

Published by ABDO Publishing Company, PO Box 398166, Minneapolis, MN 55439. Copyright © 2012 by Abdo Consulting Group, Inc. International copyrights reserved in all countries. No part of this book may be reproduced in any form without written permission from the publisher. The Essential Library™ is a trademark and logo of ABDO Publishing Company.

Printed in the United States of America,
North Mankato, Minnesota
102011
012012

♲ THIS BOOK CONTAINS AT LEAST 10% RECYCLED MATERIALS.

Editor: Lisa Owings
Copy Editor: Karen Latchana Kenney
Series and cover design: Becky Daum
Interior production: Becky Daum and Christa Schneider

Library of Congress Cataloging-in-Publication Data
Kershner, Tad, 1967-
  Living with ADHD / by Tad Kershner.
      p. cm. -- (Living with health challenges)
  Includes bibliographical references.
  ISBN 978-1-61783-122-5
  1. Attention-deficit hyperactivity disorder--Juvenile literature. I. Title.
  RJ506.H9K46 2012
  618.92'8589--dc23
                                    2011033150

TABLE OF CONTENTS

EXPERT ADVICE

Living with ADHD can be difficult, especially at school. As a licensed pediatrician, I have been working with children and teens for four years. I am currently learning how best to diagnose and treat people with ADHD. It may seem unfair that you have to work so much harder than your classmates to get decent grades. And as a high school student, you have more responsibility, more work to do, and less help to get it done. The good news is that there are many things you can do to make living with ADHD a little easier.

Get organized. Staying organized is a key to success in school and in your chosen career. It may not be easy to be organized, but you can find ways that work well for you. Experiment with different organizational methods to see what helps you stay focused.

Get involved. If you haven't already, join an activity, sport, or club that you enjoy. When you're feeling down about school, this will give you a chance to show your strengths. It also gives you an opportunity to work on skills outside the classroom.

Don't be afraid to ask for help. Everyone needs help sometimes, and there are plenty of people around who are happy to give you support when you need it. Don't be afraid to let friends, parents, or teachers know if you can't deal with your symptoms on your own.

As a teenager with ADHD, you have many options for treatment. Work with your health-care provider to find one that fits you. Remember that having ADHD doesn't mean you're not smart. I worked with a teenage boy who was very bright but still struggled with school. We diagnosed him with ADHD and found ways to help him deal with his symptoms. Now he is doing well in school, getting along with his parents, and generally enjoying life. Like that boy, you will find ways to manage your ADHD symptoms so you can thrive at school and in your personal life. Knowing what treatments are out there and whom you can talk to are the first steps toward taking control of your life.

—*Elizabeth Hastings, MD, Developmental and Behavioral Pediatrics Fellow, University of Michigan, Ann Arbor, MI*

MY LIFE ON FAST FORWARD

"Can it, Codes!"

Alex shoved him, and Cody shoved back. Across the table, Jenn giggled nervously and whispered something to her friend Mala. The girls both looked at Cody and giggled again. Cody felt that familiar roller coaster drop in his stomach as Jenn laughed at him: Jenn "the Amazing," with those amazing green eyes and that amazing bright smile. And in those jeans . . .

It wasn't supposed to go this way. Cody had begged Alex to set up the study group right before the history final. It had been the perfect excuse to spend time with Jenn and impress her with his knowledge of Renaissance art. But somehow Cody just couldn't stop talking about Leonardo Da Vinci's inventions. If he'd stopped to think about it first, he would have realized that girls don't care about ornithopters and giant crossbows. But he never stopped to think about it. He always just charged in, with his mouth on full automatic.

Jenn looked down at her notes and asked, "Does anyone know what year the Council of Trent was? I know that's gonna be on the test."

Cody's eyes lit up. He'd just studied that one last night! He shouted, "YESSS!" But as soon as he looked into Jenn's eyes, his brain shot ahead to how he was going to ask her to the prom and how it would feel to kiss her.

Council of Trent. Right. It was 15-something. Or was it 14-something?

ADHD can be frustrating, but it can also be an advantage. People with ADHD are often gifted with creativity, energy, and a great sense of humor.

"It was 1545," said Juan, grinning his big football star grin.

"Thanks!" Jenn smiled at him.

Alex gave Cody a sympathetic look. Owned by Juan Beedle in his own study group. How bad did that bite?

Why couldn't he just be normal like Juan? Cody wished that just this once, his brain would slow down to normal speed and let him focus when it was really important.

Why did he have to study all these stupid dates anyway? How was he ever supposed to learn this stuff? And how was he supposed to get Jenn to like him when he seemed so different from everyone else?

LIFE WITH ADHD

Cody's doctor calls what's going on with him ADHD, which is short for attention deficit hyperactivity disorder. At times when it seems like an impossible barrier to getting what he wants, Cody has other words for his ADHD—words that would get him in big trouble. Other times, he really loves being able to think of creative solutions to problems, do exhilarating things such as rock climbing and wakeboarding, and make hilarious YouTube videos that everyone loves.

If you have ADHD, you may feel like your brain is moving too fast. Maybe you are easily distracted and have trouble

THE TELLTALE SIGNS

Unlike asthma or diabetes, there are no definite medical tests for ADHD, but people do experience its symptoms. The symptoms of inattention/distractibility include:

- making careless mistakes
- being easily distracted
- having trouble focusing on activities
- having trouble listening
- difficulty following instructions and finishing tasks
- disorganization, losing pencils, books, or assignments

The symptoms of hyperactivity/impulsivity include:

- fidgeting or squirming
- feeling restless
- being continually on the go
- nonstop talking
- interrupting
- blurting out answers before questions are finished

focusing on one thing for any length of time. You may also be impulsive and have difficulty waiting for something you want, or perhaps you blurt things out without thinking them through. Hyperactivity—always fidgeting and hating to sit still—is also common. Not everyone with ADHD has all of these symptoms, so doctors split the symptoms into three types: inattentive/distractible (what used to just be called ADD), hyperactive/impulsive (HI), and combined type (CT).[1]

Almost everyone exhibits some of these symptoms sometimes. In order to be diagnosed with ADHD, you have to experience symptoms over a long period of time, and they have to affect multiple areas of your life.

A HISTORICAL PERSPECTIVE

ADHD symptoms have been discussed in medical literature as far back as 1798.[2] The term *ADD* was first used to describe the condition in 1980 and was officially changed to ADHD in 1987. In 1994, the symptoms were divided into three groups: inattentiveness/distractibility, hyperactivity/impulsivity, and a combination of these.

DRIVEN TO DISTRACTION

The world is a busy, distracting place. You may feel hot and sweaty or uncomfortably chilly. You may have an itch on your elbow or your nose. You may hear threads of other conversations, music, a television, sirens, or car alarms. Or you may be worrying about something that happened last week, your friends' opinions of what you're wearing, what to say to your current crush, how to get all your homework done on time, and what to eat when you get home. Like a video showroom with 20 televisions going at once, all of these things are competing for your attention.

Your brain has filters that tune out most of these distractions and help you focus on the important things. But what if your filters don't work perfectly all the time? That's what happens when you have ADHD. Without working filters, it can be impossible to focus enough to get anything done.

Think about all the pieces involved in completing just one task:

- breaking the task into steps

- putting the steps in the correct order

- tuning out everything else to focus on just one step

- completing each step

- remembering which steps have already been done

This process is so basic that most people don't even think about it, but ADHD causes changes in your brain that can turn easy tasks into big challenges. It's often difficult

PROFILE: WILL SMITH

Will Smith's teachers may not have expected him to go very far in life. Smith says:

I was the fun one who had trouble paying attention. . . . Today they'd diagnose me as a child with ADHD. . . . I was a B student who should've been getting A's—classic underachiever.[3]

Starting as a rapper with a platinum album, Smith had a hit TV show for six years and went on to star in a long string of mega-hit movies, including *Independence Day*, *Men In Black*, *Shark Tale*, and *I Am Legend*.

All of these successes were the result of years of hard work and careful planning. Smith created a strategy and used his unique talents and energy to follow it. He said, "There's nothing you've ever been successful at that you didn't work on every day."[4]

for anyone who doesn't have ADHD to understand how ADHD challenges other people. If you have ADHD, you may think it's unfair that you have to work twice as hard as others to do what seems simple to them. But do you know that you're also developing valuable skills that other people may not have? Persistence is the ability to stick with something even when faced with challenges such as living with ADHD. It is also a vital skill needed to succeed in most areas of your life. Millions of people have ADHD, and they each use different strategies to manage their symptoms. Their strategies help them lead happy and productive lives.

By discovering your own unique talents and skills, you can discover ways to excel in your life.

ASK YOURSELF THIS

- *What type of ADHD do you think Cody has? Why? How is Cody's behavior at school similar to or different from yours?*

- *What are your ADHD symptoms? Which ones affect your life the most? Do any of your symptoms have a positive effect on your life?*

- *What are some ways you can use your ADHD to your advantage?*

- *What are your top three favorite time-wasters? What do you get out of them?*

- *What are some ways you can minimize distractions in your life?*

WHY ME? CAUSES AND RISK FACTORS

"Where are you? We've been waiting online forever! We're playing the Myth Hammers tonight, remember?" Tyler's voice came accusingly out of the phone.

Amir stared down at the rows of numbers and symbols in his math textbook. "Sorry dude, if I don't finish page 97, Mr. Cook's gonna kill me," he told Tyler.

"Dude, it's way after nine. I finished hours ago."

The rows of numbers danced in Amir's head. "I'll have to catch you next time."

"If we get destroyed, it's so gonna be your fault."

Amir sighed. He knew this stuff. He should have been able to jam through it in an hour. But here it was 9:00 p.m. and he was only a quarter through. At this rate, he'd be done at around 2:00 a.m. He'd been sitting at his desk all afternoon and all he had to show for it was an empty pizza box and ten finished problems.

Why couldn't he just focus and get through his homework like everyone else?

It was all the ADHD's fault. That was what everything always boiled down to—stupid ADHD. Why did he have to get stuck with it anyway? He pictured his friends all having a blast online with their epic battle while he was stuck with a defective brain.

Amir popped open his laptop and Googled "What causes ADHD?" There were at least 8,780,000 results.

Scientific studies of twins show that having certain genes makes people more likely to develop ADHD.

As he started clicking, he grew more confused. There were links connecting ADHD to everything from TV to sugar to pesticides. Didn't anyone know why this was happening to him?

THEORIES AND MORE THEORIES

Amir is right about one thing: the number of possible causes for ADHD can certainly be bewildering. Doctors and scientists are still trying out dozens of different theories. Some seem to fit, while others are open to debate.

GENETICS

Many studies support the idea that ADHD tends to run in families. One such study found that more than 25 percent of parents, siblings, or children of people with ADHD also had the disorder, compared with only 5 percent of the general population.[1]

Identical twins share the exact same genes, and nonidentical twins do not. One intriguing study found that 82 percent of identical twins either both had or both did not have ADHD, as opposed to only 38 percent of nonidentical twins.[2] These studies strongly suggest that ADHD is hereditary.

Some children with ADHD who have a certain gene have thinner brain tissue and less

THE MASQUERADE: OTHER ISSUES THAT LOOK LIKE ADHD

Researchers say nearly 1 million children in the United States may be misdiagnosed with ADHD.[3] People with certain vision problems often have trouble paying attention for long periods. Their eyes don't work together, so words seem to move or turn blurry, making it hard to focus. People with thyroid disease are often tired, moody, and have trouble concentrating, which looks exactly like the inattentive symptoms of ADHD. Be sure your doctor also evaluates you for these and other medical conditions—such as depression, anxiety, or learning disabilities—that may be masquerading as ADHD.

activity in the areas of the brain controlling attention. However, as children with this gene grow up, their brain tissue gets thicker and their ADHD symptoms improve.

WHAT'S GOING ON INSIDE: FUN WITH BRAINS!

Our brains are extremely complicated, and scientists only recently began figuring out what may actually cause ADHD. Your brain contains billions of nerve cells, called neurons. These cells use chemicals called neurotransmitters to communicate with each other. While many brain chemicals are involved in ADHD, scientists are discovering that one, called dopamine, is especially important.

AN EVOLUTIONARY ADVANTAGE?

Many studies have shown that people with ADHD symptoms have lower dopamine levels in their brains. But is this because their bodies aren't producing normal amounts of dopamine, or because their brains need more than normal? Some intriguing studies have discovered a gene variant called DRD4, which is a dopamine receptor and seems to be more common among children with ADHD. Called the novelty-seeking gene, it appears to have evolved at the dawn of human culture and civilization.

The DRD4 gene may have provided an evolutionary advantage, as it probably made people more likely to explore new territory and find new sources of food. As the world faces new challenges in the areas of energy, the economy, and the environment, it needs people with the novelty-seeking gene more than ever!

As signals flow from your senses through your nervous system, they activate neurons in your brain. The amount of neural activity is called stimulation. A totally silent, dark room provides almost no stimulation, while a loud concert with a bright light show produces a lot of stimulation.

Dopamine levels seem to be related to the way people experience stimulation. People with ADHD appear to have lower levels of dopamine in their brains, which may create a continual thirst for outside stimulation. This idea could explain the symptoms of all three types of ADHD. The continual newness of impulsive actions, the frequent focus changes of inattention, and the constant physical motion of hyperactivity all provide stimulation that dopamine-starved brains crave. This theory also helps us understand why many classrooms aren't stimulating enough to satisfy the thirsty brains of students with ADHD.

People with ADHD could be understimulated. This may be why certain stimulant medications work well in treating ADHD. They stimulate the brain from within, which reduces the need for outside stimulation.

TOXIC SUBSTANCES

Being exposed to toxic substances may be another cause of ADHD. A mother's use of alcohol, cigarettes, or other drugs during pregnancy may lead to ADHD or ADHD-like symptoms. Some studies indicate that children whose mothers smoked during pregnancy are twice as likely to develop ADHD.[4] Children exposed to secondhand smoke in their home also have a significantly higher risk. Exposure to lead, which can be found in old water pipes, peeling paint, or toys, also heightens the risk of developing ADHD.

Many common pesticides are designed to kill insects by interfering with their brain chemistry. A recent study from the Harvard School of Public Health found a significant connection between the levels of pesticide residues ingested by children and their chances of having ADHD. These kids weren't living near chemical plants or on farms; they were just children exposed to average levels of pesticides from food and drinking water. As a result of the study, some doctors advise buying organic fruits and vegetables and washing all produce carefully to remove pesticide residues.

VIDEO GAMES, TELEVISION, AND THE INTERNET

Television, video games, and the Internet all provide highly stimulating environments that may alter children's developing brains. A growing number of studies indicate that too much exposure to this technology can lead to an inability to concentrate. It appears to be the stimulation of the bright colors and fast editing of the programs, not their content, that causes these changes. Educational shows and games seem to be as harmful as ones meant only for entertainment.

In one study, children who had more than two hours a day of screen time were one and a half to two times more likely to have short attention spans.[5] Researchers note that the

ADHD AND SLEEP DISORDERS

Think back to a time when you didn't sleep well at night, or maybe even for several nights. You probably felt more cranky and restless than usual and had a hard time concentrating. Now remember a night when you slept really well. You probably felt refreshed the next morning and ready to conquer the world.

Several studies have shown a significant correlation between ADHD and sleep disorders (SDs). Children with certain SDs are almost twice as likely to suffer from symptoms of ADHD.[6] Since people who don't get enough sleep often show ADHD-like symptoms, it may be that SDs play a part in causing ADHD. But ADHD might also cause SDs, since people with ADHD often have trouble slowing down their minds or bodies enough to fall asleep. And because many ADHD medications are stimulants, they may also make it harder for some people to sleep.

Getting the right amount of sleep helps your brain work better, strengthens your memory and immune system, and improves your general outlook on life.

rapid pace and attention-grabbing techniques used in TV shows, video games, and Web sites seem to train brains to require more constant stimulation. It seems likely that excessive media exposure could not only cause ADHD, but it could also make life harder for people who have already been diagnosed.

Although this theory is still being studied, the American Academy of Pediatrics recommends no TV viewing at all for kids under two and no more than two hours a day for older kids. Instead, they suggest that parents and children spend time on activities such as games, blocks, puzzles, and reading, which help develop increased attention spans.[7] It is difficult

TOO MUCH INFORMATION

Compared with pre-Internet society, life today involves dealing with huge increases in both the amount of information we need to digest and the amount of information we need to filter out.

In his book *The Overflowing Brain*, Dr. Torkel Klingberg uses the term *infostress* to talk about the effect.[8] He emphasizes that the amount of stress we feel when completing certain tasks is directly related to our ability to feel in control of them.

The astronauts who landed on the moon had to complete complicated tasks under extreme pressure, and their lives literally depended on it. Yet they trained for the task for years, so when the time came they felt completely in control. Training with a coach or therapist and learning the skills to deal with information overload can help you get back in control of your life too.

Reading a book instead of watching television can help you increase your attention span.

to determine a single cause for ADHD because it likely results from a combination of different factors for different people. One day, we may discover that it isn't one condition, but a group of conditions. Rather than looking back and trying to figure out what to blame, look forward to find the best way to work with your ADHD symptoms.

ASK YOURSELF THIS

- *Why is it so important to Amir to understand his ADHD? What questions do you still have about your ADHD?*

- *Do you believe that television, the Internet, or video games may lead to ADHD or make its symptoms worse? Why or why not?*

- *Which places or situations make you feel the most bored? What can you do, without being disruptive, to add stimulation to help your brain focus?*

- *Have you noticed any particular foods that seem to give you too much energy or scramble your focus? Do any foods seem to improve your focus?*

- *What advantages could ADHD-like traits have had for humans in prehistoric days? How about now?*

PROFILE: WALT DISNEY

By many accounts, Walt Disney showed many symptoms of ADHD. He was once placed in the "second dumbest" seat in the classroom, and his teachers considered him "sleepy" and "preoccupied."[9]

Before Disney, animated cartoons were short, jerky, and black-and-white. He constantly pushed his studio to break new ground, developing many of the animation techniques we use today. The Walt Disney Studios made the first color cartoon and the first full-length animated feature film. Disney went on to win 22 competitive and three honorary Oscars.[10] Between his cartoons, films, and theme parks, Disney's fertile imagination and energetic drive transformed the world of entertainment. What things could you do by harnessing your imagination and drive?

AS IF LIFE WEREN'T HARD ENOUGH: COMPLICATIONS

"**M**om's gonna kill me," sighed Hannah. It was her second time in the principal's office in two weeks. She had promised her mom she'd never end up here again. But now here she was with another detention and another broken promise. Hannah couldn't believe she'd let her mom down again, and she'd let herself down too. What was wrong with her? Why couldn't she do anything right?

It all started when Mrs. Williams was handing back papers in English. As the teacher walked around to each student, Hannah's heart beat faster. She'd been working incredibly hard on her paper for the last three weeks. She was determined to bring her grades back up and show her mom what she could really do.

The night before the paper was due, everything seemed to go wrong. Hannah couldn't find her research note cards, so she was missing half of her references for the bibliography. She stayed up so late working on the paper that she was running behind the next morning and grabbed the wrong folder.

Finally, Mrs. Williams got to her. The teacher paused for a moment and gave her the disappointed look Hannah knew so well.

There was the grade: a big red D, the plus sign pointing at her accusingly.

"D+? I worked my butt off on this paper!" Hannah's voice sounded shrill, and way too loud, but she couldn't help herself.

"I'm sorry, but you turned it in late, your bibliography was disorganized, and you had coffee stains all over your paper. You know you can do much better than this if you just apply yourself."

But another D? Hannah could feel her world crumbling.

"I HATE you! School sucks! You can all . . ." and then she'd said some really bad things.

SEVEN MYTHS ABOUT ADHD

- *Myth #1: People who have ADHD are stupid or lazy and never amount to anything.* Many famous high achievers have ADHD.
- *Myth #2: Children who are given special accommodations because of their ADHD get an unfair advantage.* People with ADHD have brains that work differently. Special accommodations help students with ADHD work with their brains instead of against them, so they can be successful.
- *Myth #3: Children with ADHD eventually outgrow their condition.* Up to 50 percent will continue to experience symptoms in adulthood.[1]
- *Myth #4: ADHD affects only boys.* While more boys are currently diagnosed with ADHD, it also impacts a large number of girls.
- *Myth #5: ADHD is the result of bad parenting.* The problem comes from brain chemistry, not a lack of discipline.
- *Myth #6: Children who take ADHD medication are more likely to abuse drugs when they become teenagers.* Having untreated ADHD increases the risk of abusing drugs or alcohol.
- *Myth #7: Medication cures ADHD.* Medication often improves symptoms, but it should be part of a full treatment plan that may include academic help and therapy.

Some people will judge you harshly because of your ADHD. Adjust your environment so you can prove them wrong.

How did she expect anyone to understand her when she couldn't even understand herself? Sweet, smart Hannah who loved painting flowers and hiking in the forest was a cool, lovable girl. So why did she turn into this raging, swearing lunatic at school?

COMPLICATIONS

Living with ADHD can be rough. Your brain seems to work differently than most, and it can be hard to separate who you are from your ADHD. If you have continual challenges, you may feel like you are defective.

Like Hannah, you may want to show your true self, but your ADHD keeps getting in the way. It might seem that no one knows who you really are underneath the chaos.

If you broke your leg and had to use crutches, no one would expect you to run charging up the stairs. Your friends would hold doors open for you, your teachers would let you sit near the aisle, and your parents would help keep clutter off the floor so you could get around the house more easily. If you have symptoms of ADHD, there are no visible signs that remind people you're having a harder time than they are.

People make judgments about who you are based on what you do. If you have trouble staying organized, they may think you're a messy person. If you have trouble sitting still, they may think you're hyper. If you have trouble focusing, they may think you're stupid or lazy. And if you're continually around the people making those judgments, you may start to believe those things yourself. Just as people on crutches or in wheelchairs need special accommodations, people with ADHD also need adjustments to help their brains work at their best.

DISTRACTIBILITY

In a stimulating world, it's vital to be able to filter out things that aren't important and tune in to those that are. School can be especially challenging for people who are distractible, since it requires tuning out everything else that's going on in the classroom and focusing only on the teacher.

At any given time, you have to deal with multiple distractions: you could be too hot or too cold, have itchy clothes or tight shoes, be listening to someone else's conversation, or be watching Zach try to flirt with Tasha. You might be thinking about last night's game or worrying about tomorrow's English test.

People with distractibility find it extra challenging to ignore those things and pay close attention to the teacher. Distractibility

PENS THAT LISTEN

It can be challenging for students with ADHD to keep up with classroom lectures and take notes at the same time. Smart pens record audio and link it up to what you're writing. Later, you can go back and tap anywhere on your notes, and the pen will play back what it recorded while you were writing. If you missed part of a lecture because the teacher was going too fast, you can go back to the approximate place in your notes and it will play back that section. Then you don't have to worry about missing anything. The pens can also download everything to your computer so you can search your notes from your keyboard.

ADHD makes life's distractions extra hard to ignore. With the right coping strategies, you can learn how to stay focused.

can also interfere with your relationships with friends and family. They may feel that you aren't listening to them or that you don't think they're important. When you enter college—and later the workforce—coping with distractions may be vital to your success.

IMPULSIVITY

People with ADHD may act quickly without thinking about the consequences. In his book *ADHD & Me: What I Learned From Lighting Fires At the Dinner Table*, Blake Taylor describes his experience of growing up with ADHD: "You shoot pebbles because you want to see them fly, and you don't think about the objects in their path."[2]

This can be especially challenging because well-meaning children with impulsivity can feel bad about breaking someone's window, and then go on to do something equally destructive because they don't think about the consequences of their actions.

Outsiders may judge this behavior as mean or irresponsible, but a person with impulsivity has trouble connecting an action to its result. Being impulsive does not mean you are a bad person. It just means you need to learn to understand how your brain works and use that information to avoid making poor decisions in the future.

HYPERACTIVITY

People with the *H* part of ADHD may find it challenging to sit still for an entire class period. Since their brains want constant physical stimulation, they may be in and out of their chairs or continually fidgeting. During school, this behavior can be very disruptive.

THE FIDGET FACTOR

Many ADHD children are given medication specifically to help them sit still so they can concentrate better. But some studies suggest that many children focus better when they are allowed to wiggle. Fidgeting may help children and adults with ADHD keep their brains tuned in to their main focus. It makes sense: if you're bored, it's hard to stay focused on anything. Physical stimulation may provide just the right amount of interest to keep your attention from straying and help you learn.

Exasperated teachers and principals may tell the student to just keep it under control, which is not always easy to do without help.

Similarly, a friend may be trying to talk to a hyperactive person about an important issue, such as bad grades, trouble with parents, or a difficult breakup. A person with hyperactivity may find it challenging to stay still and focus on his or her friend. If your friend is talking to you about an important issue and you won't stop bouncing a basketball, your friend may feel like you just don't care. Or it may be difficult for a lower-energy friend to keep up with your continual high energy. This can make friendships challenging to develop and maintain.

BOUNCING GRADES

In addition to the unique complications caused by individual symptoms of ADHD, many students across the whole spectrum of ADHD face similar challenges. Often, students with ADHD are very bright. When they are able to focus and concentrate, they can achieve high grades. Other times, their grades can be very low because they had trouble concentrating on their work, missed part of their work, or did not turn their work in on time.

These bouncing grades can cause frustrated parents or teachers to tell students

Your parents may not understand your bouncing grades. Ask them to help you develop strategies to focus better in school.

they are not living up to their potential. The response from those who don't understand ADHD is frequently to "just try harder." The truth is that students with ADHD are probably trying much harder than many of their classmates already.

If you're in this situation, talk to your parents and teachers honestly about the challenges you're facing. They may be able to help brainstorm approaches to overcoming these challenges. And they probably won't have any idea what you're going through unless you tell them.

ADOPTING A PERSONA

Sometimes dealing with these issues on a daily basis can become overwhelming. The struggle may seem too hard and the results too few. It doesn't seem worth it to keep trying and failing. Some people may become angry or decide to give up.

Often, students with ADHD will pretend to be someone else. It is hard when you try to live up to high expectations and never quite succeed. Sometimes it seems easier to pretend to be someone who just doesn't care. If the rest of the

PROFILE: ROBIN WILLIAMS

Anyone who has seen Robin Williams in a movie, as a stand-up comic, or on a talk show, will probably laugh out loud remembering the experience. The Oscar-winning actor is a comic genius. Some of his funniest moments are unscripted: directors just let him be himself and roll the cameras! He thinks extremely fast. He is also believed to have ADHD. Although he was reportedly voted least likely to succeed in high school, he has learned to channel his energy and quick mind into hilarious comedy. This brilliant actor and comedian is one of a large number of people who have learned to turn their ADHD symptoms into valuable assets.

world believes in this facade and lowers their expectations of the student, the student may feel less likely to disappoint others.

Adopting a persona of someone who doesn't care can feel like a way of protecting yourself from pain and disappointment. But you can exceed people's highest expectations just by being your true self.

ASK YOURSELF THIS

- *Have you ever been in a frustrating situation like Hannah's? What did you do?*

- *How do you deal with poor or bouncing grades? What can your teachers or parents do to help you improve them?*

- *Has someone ever treated you like you were lazy or stupid because of your ADHD? How did it make you feel? What did you do about it?*

- *What complications does ADHD cause in your life? How do you deal with these challenges? Is there a better way to cope with them?*

- *Which of the three main symptoms of distractibility, impulsivity, and hyperactivity is the most challenging for you? How come?*

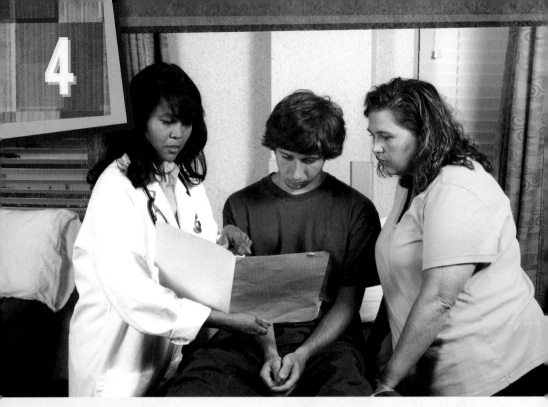

4

WELL, DO I HAVE IT? TESTS AND DIAGNOSIS

Ryan climbed to the top of the big maple tree near the bus stop. No matter how many times he'd been told not to climb up there, he still couldn't resist—especially not today, when his life was pretty much over.

Maybe not really, but he sure felt like it. If the doctor told him he really did have ADHD, he might have to go to a special school and have to quit the soccer team.

As he saw his mom's car pulling in, Ryan thought about making a run for it and sneaking home like he'd done for the last two appointments. But this time, his parents had made it clear: go or be off the soccer team.

Although Ryan always had trouble sitting still and staying focused, he fought hard to hide it. He worked like a cop watching over his own misbehaving brain. But somehow it managed to trip him up anyway, and there were the notes home and the parent-teacher conferences and the requests that he get tested for ADHD.

He wanted to be Ryan Turner, star soccer player, not Ryan Turner, ADHD burnout. So he decided to fake the test.

As he was giving the doctor all the answers he thought he wanted to hear, Ryan started wondering. Hiding it was always so hard. What if medication really could help him?

"Does this mean I'll have to go to a different school?" he asked.

The doctor smiled. "Medication may actually help you stay in regular school, if that's what you want. You know how tired you get after a good soccer game? And how you need protein and carbs to fuel your body again? Just like your body needs fuel to keep going, your brain needs chemicals for the different parts to talk to each other. The right medication can provide those chemicals or help the brain's chemicals work better.

Ryan thought about it. He could always stop taking the meds and go back to faking it again. But what if it really did make life easier?

AT THE DOCTOR'S OFFICE

There won't be needles, and you won't have to pee in a cup. Instead, your parents and teachers may be asked to fill out several checklists and questionnaires

CHECKLIST: YOUR ASSESSMENT

Here's a list of things you and your parents should bring with you to your assessment:

- a list of concerns from you, your parents, and your teachers
- two years of report cards and any notes from your school
- contact information for teachers and other adults who work with you on a regular basis
- results from any other tests you've taken (IQ tests, achievement tests, personality assessments, and any previous ADHD evaluations)
- an Individualized Education Plan (IEP) if you have one
- medical history and contact information for your pediatrician or family doctor
- insurance information

about your behavior, your strengths, and your challenges.

Getting distracted, acting impulsively, and having a lot of energy are normal parts of childhood and adolescence. Almost anybody could feel distracted and fidgety before a big game, during a long lecture, or when you're thinking about asking your crush on a date. But if these symptoms start interfering with your life over a long period of time, your teachers or parents may recommend that your doctor evaluate you for ADHD.

Since your brain is so complex, it's not simple to determine whether you have ADHD. It isn't based on medical tests. Specialists sometimes use the word *assessment* in addition to *diagnosis* to refer to the process of evaluating a person for ADHD.

Typically, you will first see your pediatrician or family doctor. That's a good place to start because he or she already knows a lot about you and your history, and may know your family or siblings as well.

Because the evaluation is subjective, a doctor or other health-care provider will need to collect a lot of information. They will want to know about your school and medical history. They will gather information from your parents and teachers. They may also contact babysitters, coaches, and other adults in your life to get as accurate a picture as possible.

They will want to know about the places you usually spend time, to see if your environment is interfering with your focus. Anyone would find it difficult to study in a messy, freezing cold room with poor light and a screaming baby next door!

The doctor will need to make sure your ADHD symptoms are not being confused with some other issue, such as vision or hearing problems, learning disabilities, anxiety, or depression. Traumatic events such as a recent illness, divorce, or death in the family can often cause ADHD-like symptoms, so a doctor will need to rule those out too.

ADHD BY THE NUMBERS

According to the US Centers for Disease Control and Prevention (CDC), in 2007:

- Boys were more than twice as likely as girls to have ADHD.[1]
- Almost one in every ten children ages 4 to 17 had been diagnosed with ADHD.[2]
- Diagnosis of ADHD increased an average of 3 percent per year from 1997 to 2006 and an average of 5.5 percent per year from 2003 to 2007.[3]

Because the diagnosis of ADHD is partially subjective, it's difficult to tell what these figures actually mean. Perhaps the incidence of ADHD is actually increasing. The increase could be due to more kids being evaluated for ADHD now. Or maybe doctors are becoming more aware of it and are more likely to make a diagnosis. Like most things about ADHD, these statistics leave many questions unanswered.

Talking to a school counselor or psychologist can help you figure out whether you might have ADHD.

Your doctor may then refer you to someone who specializes in ADHD and similar conditions. This person will have you take verbal and written tests to get a better idea of how your brain works. Finding out if you have ADHD is the first step toward successfully managing your attention and focus issues.

ASK YOURSELF THIS

- *Why was Ryan scared of going to the doctor? Can you relate to his fears? Why or why not?*

- *Would you treat someone differently if you knew he or she had ADHD? Would people treat you differently?*

- *What labels have people placed on you? How do they treat you differently because of them? How do you respond?*

IF YOU'RE TOLD YOU MIGHT HAVE ADHD

Different behaviors might indicate special abilities. Traits such as high energy, risk taking, and flexible thinking can cause challenges for children in school situations but are often assets in adult careers. To better understand ADHD, Dr. Bonnie Cramond advises to:

- Study how creativity and other special abilities might show up as ADHD behavior.
- Notice and record the conditions when key behaviors get better or worse.
- Ask: What am I thinking about while daydreaming? You may be focusing very intensely—just on something different than you are supposed to!
- Ask for a creativity assessment in addition to the ADHD evaluation.
- Choose a psychologist who is knowledgeable about giftedness and creativity as well as ADHD.
- If you have questions or doubts, get a second opinion. No doctor is perfect, and it never hurts to hear someone else's point of view.
- Find opportunities, both inside and outside of school, to exercise your creativity and build your self-esteem.[4]

- *Do you think being diagnosed with ADHD would make Ryan's life easier or harder? Should he try taking medication if it might help him focus?*

- *What methods have you tried to control distraction, impulsivity, or hyperactivity? In what ways have they worked? Not worked?*

PROFILE: GREAT INVENTORS

You probably talked on the phone, read under an electric lightbulb, and rode in a car today. You may have watched a movie or listened to an mp3 player whose great-great-grandfather was a phonograph, a device similar to a record player.

The famous inventors who made these activities possible are Thomas A. Edison, Alexander Graham Bell, and Henry Ford. All of them had many ADHD symptoms when growing up. They each learned to channel their wandering minds along innovative paths, and they dealt with hundreds of failures before perfecting the inventions that defined their lives and changed the world.

GETTING HELP: TREATMENT METHODS

isha looked at the orange prescription bottle next to her Shakespeare book. It had been her constant companion for so many years. But today was the beginning of a new adventure. She felt a little like one of those

Medication is a common treatment for ADHD, but it doesn't work for everyone. There are many alternative treatments for ADHD.

adventurers from the sixteenth century, setting sail for uncharted territory. Today, she was the uncharted territory.

When she'd last been without medication, she'd been just a girl. Now she was nearly 17. She knew a lot more about herself, and she had more self-discipline. She also had more help. Her mom and her ADHD support group were there if she needed them, and she knew she would. She had a structured schedule to keep her on track, colored blocks to build with, and classical music to listen to when her mind started wandering. She told all of her friends she wouldn't be on Facebook or IM for a month. If they wanted to talk to her, they could call her. Using a phone to talk, what a concept!

Aisha wiped the dust from the pill cutter she'd been using for a week to help her taper off her dosage. Dr. Rogers had warned Aisha about how sick she'd get if she didn't go off her meds slowly, and she didn't want to start her experiment that way.

In the last few months, she'd been reading a lot of books about ADHD and talking to her friends who had it. Some of them loved their meds, some hated them, and some didn't take them. Trying to make sense of all the arguments had been confusing.

So, Aisha talked it over with Dr. Rogers.

"You aren't any of your friends," he'd said. "You aren't any of the people in the books. We'll have to see what works for you and then decide." That was the start of her great experiment.

Aisha drew a tall sailing ship on the front of her binder. It would help keep her focused on the adventure during the hard work ahead. Whatever happened, it was only an experiment. Together, she, her parents, and Dr. Rogers would decide what to do next.

THE COST OF STABILITY

Some experts wonder if the price for suppressing ADHD symptoms with medication may be too high. They point to the great scientists, artists, inventors, and entrepreneurs with symptoms and wonder what these people would have been like without the characteristics that made them unique. Yes, medication makes things easier for students and teachers today. But is society losing the geniuses of tomorrow? Some people feel that medication has restored sanity to their lives. Others try medication, but give it up because they feel it stifles their creativity. In the end, it has to be your decision.

MEDICATION

Many people with ADHD take regular medication for it. A doctor with a diabetic patient can run blood tests that determine what type of medication to prescribe and how much. Since brain chemistry is so complex, a doctor may need to try different ADHD

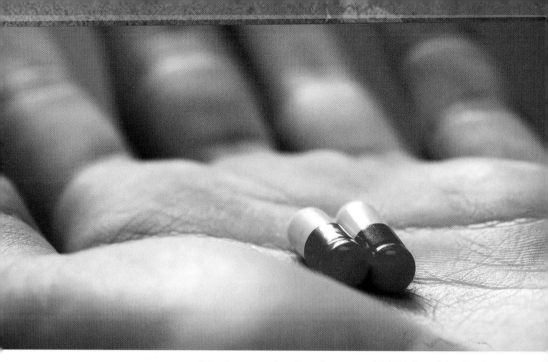

Starting medication for your ADHD is a big deal. Be sure to consult with your doctor regularly and carefully monitor changes in your symptoms.

medications to find the one that works best for you, and the dosage may need adjustment over time.

If you choose to try medication, everything may work perfectly right out of the gate, or it may take a little longer to fine-tune the right medication and dosage for you. During this period, you can help your doctor find the best match. Watch yourself closely to see how each medication affects you. Take specific notes. Which symptoms seem to improve? Does it seem to make anything worse? Do you notice any side effects, such as feeling more depressed or angry than usual? Since it may not be easy to distinguish normal mood swings from side effects, enlist outside help. Ask your parents, your close friends, and anyone else you trust to tell you if they notice you being unusually moody, emotional, or depressed.

Some people experience other side effects, such as insomnia, loss of appetite, weight loss, muscle tics, anxiety, OCD symptoms, headaches, or stomachaches. These symptoms usually go away within a few weeks. In certain cases, there can be serious heart complications. If you already have heart issues or have a family history of heart disease, be sure to mention these facts to your doctor before starting a medication. Also, people with certain mental conditions, such as bipolar disorder, may have severe reactions, so they need to be very cautious.

Review your notes about side effects with your doctor and don't be afraid to speak out, especially if your medication seems to make you depressed or angry. These kinds of side effects are not usually serious, but they need to be watched.

AVOIDING COMPLICATIONS

Many people do well with a single medication. In some cases, children can be prescribed one medication, then another to suppress the side effects of the first, and so on. Some children experiencing severe complications were found to be on several very strong medications from multiple doctors who were not communicating with each other.

Some doctors may have a large number of patients, so they can't spend as much time as they would like to study each case thoroughly. You and your family have the most time to follow your situation. Be as informed as you can, and be active in your own care. Read the information booklets provided with each drug thoroughly. Ask questions about any concerns you have.

Study articles from reputable sources about different medications. Pay close attention to any drug interactions. Be especially cautious if you are prescribed more than one medication, especially if one is to deal with the side effects of another. If you have more than one doctor, make sure they each know your complete

PROFILE: GREAT ARTISTS

Vincent Van Gogh lived from 1853 to 1890 and is famous for the vivid colors and emotional impact of his paintings. Pablo Picasso (1881–1973) was both a painter and a sculptor. He is best known for his experimental work.

As children, these brilliant artists did not fit in well with the world around them. By many experts today, they are considered to have had ADHD. Their unique artistic styles have had an immeasurable effect on the evolution of art. Many art historians argue that their art would have been neither as good nor as revolutionary if they had not had ADHD symptoms.

IEPs and 504 plans can help you get the individual guidance you need to be successful in school.

medical history, including all medications you are currently taking.

Make sure that you and your parents read up on the pros and cons of any medication before you decide whether to take it. It's a big decision, so you and your parents should make it carefully. Don't let anyone pressure you into something you're not comfortable with. It's your ADHD and your decision!

SCHOOL ACCOMMODATIONS

Your parents and your school may work together to design a plan to help you succeed at school. A 504 plan provides adjustments such as allowing you to sit away from a noisy air conditioner so you can concentrate better, or go to the nurse's office during class to take medication. Or you might have an individualized education plan (IEP), which tailors your classes and workload to fit your specific strengths and challenges.

An IEP will include a list of accommodations, such as receiving extra time on tests, written study guides before tests, additional time with homework, or any other changes that might help you. It includes a section for daily, monthly, and yearly goals, which may be as simple as raising your hand rather than blurting out answers in class, or as involved as learning to read at grade level by the end of the year. IEPs are typically reviewed each year and adjusted to account for any significant changes.

OTHER APPROACHES

Many doctors report great success with different programs they have created for working with ADHD without medication. Look at the credentials of the people who created the programs. What are their success rates? What research do they use to back up their programs? Are they well documented and reviewed? Are there independent testimonials? Do the programs offer anyone you can speak with personally? Can you try the program at home cheaply or do you have to attend a series of long-term and expensive visits? Do the programs make money from selling products or supplements? With careful research and observation—and a healthy dose of trial and error—you'll be able to find a treatment method that works for you.

ART THERAPY

Many experts believe that creative activities such as drawing, painting, dancing, or making music really help people with ADHD. Listening to classical music seems to make it easier to concentrate, even for people without symptoms. Art therapy is a recognized and licensed branch of mental health counseling that uses art in all its forms to help people. It may prove to be one of the most effective methods to help people regain focus in their lives.

Art and art therapy can provide a refuge from the overly stimulating world. Making art allows you to focus on simple, enjoyable activities that relax your mind and alleviate your stress in the moment. There is also evidence that art therapy provides long-term benefits.

ASK YOURSELF THIS

- *Why do some people love their medication and some people hate it?*

- *What treatment methods would you like to explore? How will you make a decision about which type of treatment is right for you? Who can help you make this decision?*

- *Have you tried any approaches to ADHD treatment that weren't discussed in this chapter? How did they work for you?*

- *Why was it so important for Aisha to have support during her experiment? Who do you feel supports you?*

- *Why do you think some ADHD treatments are so controversial?*

MAKING YOUR LIFE WORK: COPING STRATEGIES

It's way too quiet in the room: all the students can hear is the whir of the heating fan and the scratching of their pencils across their exam booklets.

When it's this quiet, Sara's mind wanders everywhere but where it should be. Of course,

*Once you learn to work with your ADHD instead of
against it, you may be surprised at how much you
can accomplish.*

when it's too loud, her mind follows every little
sound.

But whining about it won't get her the car for
Christmas.

If she can bring her GPA up to a 3.5 this
semester, she'll get the keys to the funky old
Mustang that's been sitting in their driveway for
the last month.

She's busted her butt in every other class.
Now if she aces the English final, she'll have
the car.

She grips her pencil so hard it almost
breaks. She knows her thesis by heart: "Envy
and Ambition vs. Honor and Patriotism." It's just
a matter of connecting the dots—one idea to the
next idea, and then on to the next. A to B to C to
D. She's rehearsed this so many times.

Now her mind is off again, thinking about
the snow on the pass, and whizzing full
speed down the hill on her new skis. For the
thousandth time she brings her mind back to her
point. She's underlined it on her scratch paper
so she knows which one to stay on. All the
points she's already made are crossed off.

Sara writes one more sentence and takes
a sip of water—a sentence and then a sip. She
lets herself draw one tree in the scene on her
scratch paper. She's set this up carefully. Each

sentence gets its own reward, and each reward keeps her focused.

A week later, when her dad hands her the official-looking envelope from the school with all of her graded finals in it, she goes into instant panic mode. What if she forgot one of her key points? What if she didn't make the logic clear enough? Fortunately, she only needs a B.

She thumbs through the other papers until she finds her English final. Mr. Olive's note on the top takes a moment to register: "Incredible job. You should be a writer!"

Sara can't keep herself from a little whoop of triumph. Her parents sweep her into a big hug, and she can hear the jingle of the car keys already.

COPING STRATEGIES

When you're frustrated by your ADHD—whether your grades aren't what you want them to be, you keep losing things, or you just can't stay focused—it may sound like a good idea to make a resolution never to let yourself get distracted again. But just like people on a diet who tell themselves they'll never eat ice cream again, that's just not realistic. Instead of making the impossible your goal, set yourself up to succeed by using a few simple coping strategies, such as changing your diet, exercising regularly, and adding structure to your life.

YOUR DIET

Changing your diet just a little bit can do a lot to improve your ADHD symptoms. Take time in the morning to eat a balanced, nutritious breakfast. If you're running late, you may be tempted to skip breakfast. But having a nutritious breakfast helps fuel your brain so you can focus better throughout the day.

Limit your sugar intake. Everyone has noticed that eating sugar makes you feel hyper and happy. But it often leaves people feeling tired and depressed shortly afterward. This is because eating sugar or simple carbohydrates makes your blood sugar levels spike up and then crash down. You can balance your blood sugar by avoiding sugary foods and eating complex carbohydrates together with the right amount of protein. It's important for people with ADHD symptoms to maintain steady blood sugar levels.

DRINK PLENTY OF WATER

Drinking enough water is especially vital for people with ADHD symptoms. Every organ in your body uses water, including your brain. If you start getting dehydrated, neurons in your brain can't communicate as easily, and it's easier to become distracted. Drink at least eight to nine cups of water a day, and don't wait until you're thirsty. Thirst means you're already dehydrated.[1]

Martial arts, such as karate, kung fu, judo, aikido, and jujitsu, are integrated with mental and spiritual practices.

Watch out for allergens and artificial ingredients. Some studies have shown that artificial food additives and dyes cause ADHD-like symptoms in some children. Other children may be allergic or reactive to foods such as dairy products, wheat, and eggs. Removing allergens seems to improve ADHD symptoms for many people. You can experiment by eliminating certain foods for a while to see if it makes any difference in your symptoms. A doctor or certified nutritionist can help you use an elimination diet to determine if you might have unknown allergies.

EXERCISE

Regular exercise is especially important for people with ADHD symptoms. Physical activity increases levels of dopamine, serotonin, and norepinephrine: three major brain chemicals that affect mood, focus, and attention. Increased levels of these chemicals can also help relieve

MARTIAL ARTS, YOGA, AND DANCE

Martial arts may make you think of Jackie Chan and Jet Li movies. It turns out that taking classes in martial arts has huge benefits for many people with ADHD symptoms. Martial arts and other physical activities, such as dance and yoga, increase brain chemicals linked to concentration and mental capacity. They also help relieve stress and frustration and decrease compulsiveness and hyperactivity. Martial arts classes teach self-discipline and respect, which can have great benefits even outside the class.

Such activities help you develop control over your body and mind, which is vital for all areas of your life. They can also be a lot of fun, and you can be proud of the skills you learn from all your hard work. Team sports can be great at building cooperation skills, but having a place to achieve personal success can be very important for people with ADHD.

stress and frustration. A fourth brain chemical called BDNF is also released during exercise and helps increase concentration and mental capacity.

Exercise doesn't have to be boring. Make it fun! Pick exercises that you enjoy. There are lots of great ways to get exercise: running, biking, fencing, weight lifting, dancing, yoga, or martial arts.

STRUCTURE AND ROUTINE

Imagine being alone in a strange city, surrounded by unfamiliar sights, sounds, and people. You're supposed to meet your friend at his house, but you only know his address. Now imagine that someone handed you a GPS with your friend's address already in it—"Turn right on Fourth Street. Walk two blocks. Then turn left on Main Street."

Being able to follow a list of clear instructions in a specific order makes it easier to get where you want to go. It also allows you to relax. Similarly, having a regular routine to follow helps you accomplish what you want and makes your day go more smoothly, especially when you're coping with the added challenges of ADHD.

STRUCTURE

You wake up early on a Saturday morning with a whole free weekend ahead of you. Sure you've got a couple hours of homework, but that'll be easy. There's plenty of time to get it in, plus a couple of fun projects you want to do and some free time to just relax. Then somehow it's Sunday night and you didn't finish either the homework or the fun projects. Where did all the time go?

When you are living with ADHD, it can be especially hard to ignore all of life's distractions and buckle down when you need to. Having a regular schedule or routine helps your brain focus on one thing at a time.

TOOLS: LISTS, LISTS, LISTS!

Make a list of everything you need to get done. All those to-do's rattling around in your head are distracting, and worrying you might forget one of them is stressful. Getting your to-do's out of your brain and onto paper frees you to focus on other things. It also lets you relax because you know you won't forget them. Everyone uses lists, not just people with ADHD.

TOOLS: TIME BLOCKS

If someone put a whole birthday cake in front of you, how would you eat it? You could just slam your face into it and start eating, but maybe you'd rather cut yourself a small slice. Similarly, it's easier to maintain focus when you divide tasks on your list into manageable slices.

If you have a paper to write, you might start by dividing it into steps: research, outline, first draft, second draft, and final draft. You might need to divide each of those into smaller steps until you get something that feels manageable. Your teacher or parents can help you.

Once you've divided your work into pieces, divide your day into pieces in the same way. You could divide your day into one-hour blocks, half-hour blocks, or blocks even shorter than that depending on your needs and your plan for the day. Fit each work block into a reasonable day block and then you're set.

Don't schedule too much work time without adding something fun, though! Not only do little rewards give you something to look forward to, but the serotonin boost also helps your brain focus for your next work block.

Be sure your rewards are good for you, like a fun

MIND MAPPING

When you're reading a textbook or studying, does your mind get stuck on a mass of words that seem to blur into a puddle of gray? To solve this issue, many people use a special kind of diagram called a mind map. Using colors, pictures, and visual layouts helps stimulate your brain and makes it easier to understand and remember key concepts. It also makes studying easier and more fun.

To make a mind map, get three to four different colored pens or pencils. Take a piece of blank paper and write the main topic in the very center. Then draw branches off of it for each subtopic, and branches off the subtopics for ideas about them, and so on. Get as creative as you want with colors, drawings, and line styles. It's also a great brainstorming tool—I used mind maps to write much of this book!

Start each day by making a plan or schedule for how you want your day to go. This will help you increase your focus, reduce stress, and feel in control.

puzzle or a quick judo practice, not something that leads to more distractions. Schedule these reward blocks between your work blocks so you can give yourself a break without getting off track.

Discuss your schedule with your family. Tell them when you'll be available to talk and when you'll be focusing on your schoolwork. Make sure your parents keep your siblings from barging in on you during work blocks. And ask your parents to not discuss chores or homework with you in the middle of your reward blocks. Schedules are a vital part of getting things done, and your parents should respect that too.

TOOLS: MAKE YOUR WORKSPACE WORK FOR YOU

Try to have a regular place to work at home that's free from distractions. Go through your five senses, searching for sneaky focus stealers. Is the space crammed with clutter? Can you see the TV? Are there loud noises such as kids playing outside or repetitive ones such as a dripping faucet? Is your chair comfortable? If you have trouble sitting still, you might try a special rounded cushion that lets you rock gently while you sit. Is it too warm or too cold? Are there bad smells from the garbage can or good smells from the kitchen? Is there a candy dish or a giant bag of chips that's just too tempting?

Go down your list and resolve everything you can. Spend ten minutes

THE COLOR OF FOCUS

You already know that bright colors stimulate your mood and calming colors relax it. But did you know that colors can ease symptoms of ADHD and help you focus?

Having a small stack of colored blocks that you can build with while you think can improve your concentration. Use them at home while you study, and ask your teachers if you can use them in class without disturbing anyone. Using colored pencils or pens to take notes helps you gain focus while writing and stay focused while studying. Using different colors when you're brainstorming or mind mapping helps stimulate your creativity.

clearing your space, find a place away from the TV, get some earplugs or ask your parents to fix the faucet, grab a pillow to sit on, and move the chips and candy. You may not be able to eliminate all your distractions, but do the best you can and use your creativity to improvise solutions.

TOOLS: GOOD DISTRACTIONS

You know that you are easily distracted, but are you aware of what distracts you? Make a list of all your distractions. Do you love surfing the Internet? Drawing in your sketchbook? Watching funny videos? Taking walks outside?

Go down your list and mark which ones you really enjoy, and which are just junk food for your brain. What do you get out of each of them? You wouldn't be doing them unless

YOUR BRAIN ON HUMOR

When you're stressed, worried, or anxious, you may feel like it's harder to think. But did you know that it really is? Many studies have shown that anxiety can take over the parts of your brain that are used for memory and math problems, making these thoughts much more difficult.

Humor increases brain chemicals associated with pleasure and decreases those associated with stress. It also helps loosen the grip of worry on your brain. When faced with a particularly challenging assignment, some people like to wear a silly hat or shirt, or put funny pictures by their workspace to remind themselves not to take anything too seriously.

you got something out of them. Maybe you feel lonely when you're studying so you have five chat windows open. Maybe reading about your favorite sports team lets you fantasize about being out on the field instead of stuck at the books.

See if you can substitute something from your "really enjoy" list for each thing on your "junk food" list. If you have too much on your junk food list, make another list of things you are passionate about. Do you love sports? Hiking? Horses? Clothes? Art? If you're an artist, use your time to browse art or photography Web sites or look for new music instead.

Now schedule some of your positive distractions in short time blocks as rewards. Give them a defined and contained time to happen so they don't take over your life.

TOOLS: MAKING WORK FUN

When you're bored, your brain is partially switched off, so just studying harder doesn't make much difference. Having fun wakes up your brain and makes your endorphins flow, which makes it easier to learn.

Any time you have a task you don't particularly like, it will go faster and work better if you turn it into something you can enjoy. If you have to memorize a list of 30 vocabulary words, write a story with them. Turn your work into music, drawings, or whatever suits your personality or interests.

If you have a big test on the Civil War, try writing a song with funny rhymes for the names and dates. During the test, you can sing it back to yourself. Or maybe create a sprawling drawing with all the important details in crazy colors that you can visualize later.

Have fun with your work! Not only does enlisting your creativity give your distracted mind something to focus on, but using fun and humor and engaging as many senses as possible helps cement details and makes them easier to remember later.

ME AND MY ADHD: GETTING CREATIVE

There are probably things you really love about your ADHD and things you really can't stand. But it's an important part of you, and denying it won't make it go away. Get creative to express how you feel.

Pick a form of artistic expression that works for you. Some people journal or blog to express themselves. Some people write music, songs, or skits. And some make paintings, drawings, or videos. Try a few different creative activities and continue with the ones you enjoy most.

For many people, song lyrics are easier to memorize than lists of facts. Writing a catchy song is a fun, creative way to cram for your next big test.

PLAY TO YOUR STRENGTHS, SUPPORT YOUR WEAKNESSES

We may expect ourselves to be good at everything all the time, but the truth is that everyone has different strengths and weaknesses. If you try to be perfect at everything, you will be pretty miserable, and you might not get your work done on time. Instead, learn how to play to your strengths and support your weaknesses.

What are you really good at? What areas are more of a challenge for you? If you like to look at the big picture and your friend is good at focusing on small details, maybe you could form a study group together. For

PROFILE: GREAT THINKERS

"Logic will get you from A to B. Imagination will take you everywhere."[2]

—*Albert Einstein*

Even Albert Einstein, one of the greatest geniuses of all time, had symptoms of ADHD. He struggled in school. His speech was severely delayed, and his teachers thought he was borderline mentally disabled. Yet it was his unique combination of creativity and mathematical ability that changed the world of physics and our understanding of the universe.

Einstein is best known for his work on nuclear energy, but every time you use an automatic door or faucet, make a phone call, or take a picture with your phone or digital camera, you're using his discoveries about converting light into electricity.

Find a friend whose strengths complement your weaknesses. Chances are you can achieve something great together.

example, if you're studying a war, you could help your friend remember the reasons behind the war and the general troop movements. Your friend could tutor you on the exact dates and locations of particular battles.

SOMETIMES NOTHING WORKS

Some days, despite your best intentions and hard work, nothing works right. You can't focus or sit still. Forgive yourself. Dealing with symptoms of ADHD can be hard. Remember, your life is a marathon, not a sprint. You're in it for the long haul. Everyone has a few bad days now and then. What's important is moving forward over time, not being perfect every single day. The only way to fail is to give up, and you're more likely to give up if you're always down on yourself. So give yourself a break, jot down a quick list of some things you might do better next time, and relax about it. Tomorrow is a new day.

ASK YOURSELF THIS

- *Try doing a few exercises before sitting down to work. Do you find it helps you focus better? What physical activities do you most enjoy?*

- *What are your favorite types of creative activities? How can you use them to make your tasks more enjoyable?*

- *What do you have trouble forgiving yourself for? Why? What would it mean if you could forgive yourself for these things?*

- *Design an ideal home workspace for yourself. Where is it? What does it look, smell, and feel like? What's in it?*

- *What strategies do you currently use to cope with your ADHD? Which strategies are the most helpful? Which are the least helpful?*

7

STANDING TOGETHER: GIVING AND GETTING SUPPORT

"**Y**ou just don't understand!" Becca threw down her paintbrush and stormed out of the classroom. Her best friend Andrea followed after her. "I was only saying, you can do better if you just try

*Millions of people around the world suffer from
ADHD. You are sure to find someone who
understands what you're going through.*

a little harder. I know you can. You're so smart,
Beccs!"

Becca ran down the stairs, fighting back
tears. "Just leave me alone!"

When she couldn't run anymore, she
flopped down on the steps near the music hall,
burying her head in her hands.

She thought she was too mad to cry, but the
tears came anyway.

"Hey."

She looked up to see Morgan Johnson
leaning against the wall, holding his guitar.

Great. The last person she wanted to see
was Morgan the Spaz.

"It's so easy for her!" Becca sobbed. "She
doesn't know anything!"

Why was she telling Morgan this?

He strummed a chord on his guitar.
"Sometimes the same thing happens to me
during a big test. I know that I know all the stuff
because I studied my butt off. But the facts just
buzz around inside my head like a big swarm of
bees and I can't catch any of them."

He flopped down next to her. "Then my
parents say I can't go to practice because I
didn't study enough. It makes me so mad, like
they think I'm doing it on purpose!" he said.

Becca knew exactly what that was like. She had always blown Morgan off because he was so annoying in class. It never occurred to her that he might be having the same problems she was.

Becca sniffed and wiped her eyes. "I know, right? The answers are just sitting out there, and the harder you reach for them, the farther away they fly."

"It's like they're just sticking their tongues out at you." He stuck his tongue out at her.

Becca giggled.

Morgan laughed and blew a lock of hair out of his face.

Why had she never realized how cute he was?

WORKING MEMORY

Working memory is like the brain's scratch pad. It stores instructions or other information that it currently needs. Many people with ADHD seem to have smaller areas of working memory. Teachers often fire off a long list of instructions. Students with ADHD have room to fit only a few of them in their heads at once, so they may lose their place in the middle and end up stuck, wondering desperately what to do.

Teachers and parents who understand these challenges can help greatly by giving directions in shorter bursts. You can help yourself by offloading your working memory onto a list and then crossing off items as you do them.

PEOPLE WHO DON'T GET YOU

It can be hard when your friends don't understand you or don't believe your disorder is real. Imagine your ADHD as a color other people just don't see. It would be pretty difficult trying to explain your color. Even your best friend would have a hard time understanding what you were talking about and would probably think you were a little bit crazy. Your friends who can't see your disease might think you are imagining things or just making excuses. They might not understand why you are having trouble, and they might tell you to just work harder.

PEOPLE WHO DO GET YOU

What if you suddenly found a group of people who could see your color? It would probably

CHECKLIST: FRIENDS WITH ADHD

If you don't have ADHD, you probably have a friend who does. Sometimes having friends with ADHD isn't easy. You may be trying to tell them about something that's really important to you, and they seem to be paying attention to everything but what you're saying.

- Be honest with them about your feelings. Just because they have ADHD doesn't mean they should treat you badly!
- Let them know when you feel hurt by their actions that may be related to their ADHD.
- List their behaviors that really get to you. What might make it easier to accept some of them? Which ones could you ask them to work on?
- Make your friend feel appreciated. What do you love about his or her personality? What makes that person a great friend?

If you haven't already, talk to your teachers about your ADHD symptoms. Ask for extra help outside of class when you feel you are falling behind.

be a huge relief to discover you really weren't crazy. If you take a good look around, you might be surprised at how many other people have challenges similar to yours. Maybe even some of your teachers or other adults you know have ADHD. There are many support groups for people with ADHD, and you can find them easily in the phone book or online.

Talk to people you trust. You may discover that someone else has the perfect solution to a problem that's been bugging you for a long time, or you may have a great fix for another person's problems. Some of your teachers might be glad to share their stories about coping skills they developed and how they use them as an adult. You might find friends in unlikely places.

SUPPORT

Having ADHD doesn't mean you're broken, and it's a lot of work to hide it all the time. Talk openly with people you can trust about your feelings and theirs. It's important to blow off steam sometimes and allow yourself to rant about how hard it can be. It's equally important to let people close to you know when you're having a hard time so they can help you overcome your challenges. Your family and friends are your most important support system, and they will do their best to be there for you. Don't be afraid to reach out to them when you need help.

Everyone feels down sometimes, but if you're feeling really down for a long period of time or start having suicidal thoughts, get help immediately! Talk to your school's counselor or call a suicide hotline.

ACCEPTING DIVERSITY

For a long time, people assumed there was one type of normal brain. Scientists and researchers are now discovering huge differences in people's brains, even among people with ADHD. Thomas Armstrong, expert on learning and human development, said,

> We need to admit that there is no standard brain, just as there is no standard flower, or standard cultural or racial group, and that, in fact, diversity among brains is just as wonderfully enriching as biodiversity and the diversity among cultures and races.[1]

Until the latter part of the twentieth century, most buildings were designed with little thought for people in wheelchairs. Similarly, most schools and workplaces have been designed by people whose brains work a certain way, without regard for people whose brains work differently. Today, we are learning to accept the fact that

A MULTIDIMENSIONAL APPROACH

Many experts believe that reducing a person to a single diagnosis of either having ADHD or not is too limiting. It's like getting a single grade for all of your classes instead of a full report card. Not only does collapsing the whole thing into a single grade give a limited view of what's going on, but it also makes it hard to see areas in which you really excel and areas that may need a little more work.

each person learns in a different way and faces unique challenges.

It may be difficult for people to understand how ADHD affects the way a person's brain works. You can help raise awareness of ADHD by teaching others what you know about it. Finding other people with ADHD can also be important. Look for ADHD support groups in your area if you don't already know someone who shares your symptoms. People whose brains work in similar ways have a lot to offer each other, if only to say, "You're not so strange. I've been there too, and we can get through it together."

PROFILE: GREAT PRESIDENTS

"We need [people] who can dream of things that never were." [2]

—*John F. Kennedy*

As the thirty-fifth president of the United States from 1961 to 1963, John F. Kennedy led the country through a turbulent period in its history. He was instrumental in passing new civil rights laws, and he set the ambitious goal of landing astronauts on the moon before the end of the 1960s. Kennedy was a powerful leader, known for his courage and a strong determination that earned the respect of even his most persistent critics. Most people would never suspect that he may have had ADHD.

Diversity in brain structure and learning styles is the reason two heads are better than one.

ASK YOURSELF THIS

- *Why was it so hard for Andrea to understand Becca?*

- *Who in your life has a hard time understanding you? What do you do when they just don't understand?*

- *How does your family support you when you are struggling with your ADHD? What else could they do to help you? Would you feel comfortable asking them to help you with these things?*

- *What do you think other people think of you? What if they didn't really think that at all?*

- *In what ways are your ADHD symptoms like seeing a color other people can't see? How does it make it difficult to communicate with them sometimes? What other metaphors could you use to help them understand?*

8

LOVING YOUR ADHD

"Crank it, Codes!"
Alex had to yell to be heard above the thumping beat. He pressed through the moving bodies crowding the stage.

Learn to love your ADHD by finding something that your ADHD symptoms allow you to excel at.

Cody notched up the volume and switched his laptop to a new light show. Instantly, bright, swirling, pulsing colors filled three giant screens set up across the gym. He grinned, soaking up everyone's excitement. There was more than one solution to every problem.

For months, he'd dreamed about asking Jenn to the dance, but he couldn't get up his nerve to do it. So he decided to DJ instead. He channeled all of his energy and creativity into setting up the dance.

After a frantic day of getting everything set up perfectly, Alex had brought him a pizza. "Dude! Don't tell me you can't focus on anything. When you put your mind to it, you can really buckle down."

Alex was right. Cody had worked the entire day, and he hadn't gotten distracted once. He'd even forgotten to break for lunch. Maybe if there were a way he could make studying more interesting, school would be easier too. Maybe he didn't have to let his ADHD keep him down forever.

Cody's pulse pounded in time with the beat. He leaned into the microphone. "Allllll Riiiiiiight! How are we feeeeelin'?"

His voice boomed across the gym and was echoed by loud cheers from the crowd. "How do you like this one, Springfield High?"

Cody put on a new track. The room glowed with a million lights and colors, moving to the music. The crowd cheered again and bounced to the rhythm. Cody danced along with them, feeding off their energy.

"Hey!" Jenn and Mala crowded close to the stage. Jenn was wearing an amazing red dress. She was yelling something up at him.

"Hey, you rock!" She yelled something else, which Cody couldn't hear.

He leaned in closer. "What?"

"I said, will you DJ my birthday party next month?"

FINDING YOUR ADVANTAGES

Creative people can often turn what seems to be a disadvantage into an advantage.

Cody took all the things he thought of as ADHD defects—his high bursts of energy, inability to focus on things that don't interest him, and his need for constant stimulation—and channeled them into something he was really good at.

Most people can go to the dance. Only a few people can be a great DJ. When Cody decided to start working with his ADHD instead of against it, he took a big step toward creating a successful life for himself. People who use their unique characteristics to their advantage produce great ideas, great art, great solutions, and great businesses.

Cody may not become a professional DJ, but he can have a lot of fun with it, and he's already learned the skill of capitalizing on his one-of-a-kind abilities and talents. This skill will help him succeed in his career and throughout

WORDS TO LIVE BY

"The best success stories are about people who have refused to be anyone but themselves."[1]

—*Dr. Mel Levine,* Ready or Not, Here Life Comes

"Imagination is more important than knowledge. Knowledge is limited. Imagination encircles the world."[2]

—*Albert Einstein*

"You're only given a little spark of madness. You mustn't lose it."[3]

—*Robin Williams*

"AD/HD makes simple tasks like returning phone calls or emails and paying bills more difficult for me . . . but . . . it's part of me and I'm proud of who I am. There are always things I need to improve, but the energy and charisma that are also part of having ADD make me who I am and have helped me in my sport."[4]

—*Cammi Granato, Olympic gold medalist and captain of the US women's hockey team*

"Learning about this strength, my limitation, my disorder, (ADD) forced a decision-making process that changed my life—resulting in both personal and business success."[5]

—*Michael Zane, entrepreneur and former CEO, Kryptonite Bicycle Locks*

THE IMPORTANCE OF SUCCESS

People need to feel good about themselves. Those who feel successful and believe in themselves can accomplish things no one else believes are possible. **Likewise, people who feel like failures will always struggle no matter how smart or capable they really are.**

Some students whose brains fit in well with their school's model of teaching get plenty of success and feel great about school. Others, who feel like they are continually struggling and getting nowhere, may dislike school because they have such a hard time succeeding in it. If your school's model is challenging for you, try to find ways you can adjust it to fit you better, or see if there might be a different school that already fits your learning style.

his life. What are some ways you can make the most of your unique talents? How do you stand out? What are you super good at? ADHD may be one label people have put on you. Try some others.

CREATIVE

Psychologist and author of *The Gift of ADHD*, Lara Honos-Webb says, "While the A students are learning the details of how plants make energy from sunlight, the ADHD kids are staring out the window and wondering if it still works on a cloudy day."[6]

Having ADHD may make it harder to function in school, but the ability to think creatively and combine ideas in new ways is highly valuable as an adult. If people only

People with ADHD tend to be more creative than average. Exploring your own creative talents can boost your confidence and relieve stress.

ever learned what was already known without ever exploring or asking questions, we'd never discover or invent anything new.

An ADHD person's drive to seek out new ideas may allow him or her to see patterns or connections that no one else could, leading that person to solve tough scientific problems, create new inventions, power innovative businesses, or think up catchy advertising campaigns.

CREATIVE FOCUS

Your brain is so creative that it's always looking for something to do. If you don't have anything productive to focus on, your brain will seek stimulating activities that waste your time and wreck your focus. So give it something good instead. Inexpensive puzzles and games can let your brain rest after a period of hard studying and give it good stimulation at the same time. Try something colorful, hands-on, and offline: games such as Blockhead™, ColorKu™, or even multi-colored marbles or blocks. Nurturing a plant or watching fish can also help your brain relax and concentrate on healthy things.

HYPERFOCUSED

Many people labeled with ADHD are extraordinarily good at paying attention to things they're passionate about. They can spend hours painting, dancing, playing sports, or working on science projects. This kind of prolonged attention—where a person loses track of time and the world seems to disappear except for one thing—is called "hyperfocus." Rock climbers who scale rugged peaks and surgeons who operate in daylong procedures share this ability.

People with ADHD symptoms are good at paying attention to many things in a short time, and they can also stay focused on one really interesting thing for a long time.

In many ways, people with these styles of attention don't have an attention deficit at all.

People with ADHD often report they are most calm when engaging in an activity that requires intense focus, such as rock climbing.

They just have different styles of attention than most standard schools are built for. What does your style of attention let you do or notice?

EXUBERANT AND DRIVEN

ADHD may make it hard to sit still in school, but to invent new things and create new businesses, you need endless energy, enthusiasm, and drive. Thomas Edison, who tried unsuccessfully for many years to invent an electric lightbulb, said, "If I find 10,000 ways something won't work, I haven't failed. I am not discouraged, because every wrong attempt discarded is just one more step forward."[7] Your ADHD can give you the energy to keep trying to meet your goals, even after most others would have given up.

Like many things in life, it's all about balance. Many students in school haven't yet discovered good ways to utilize their

PROFILE: ENTREPRENEURS

Relaxing airline passengers . . . with purple lighting? Running a commercial fleet . . . of spaceliners? Flying around the world . . . in a balloon? Getting married . . . on your own island? Exploring the ocean . . . in a personal submarine? The list of unusual ideas from the mind of billionaire Sir Richard Branson goes on.

Branson says he was a slow learner and could barely read when he was eight. He was (and still is) described as high-spirited, headstrong, and a handful due to his ADHD symptoms. Branson's combination of unconventional ideas, instinctual understanding of the business world, and ability to channel his boundless energy, are a brilliant formula for success.

*If your ADHD symptoms continue into adulthood,
use the strategies you've learned in this book
to cope through college and your career.*

ADHD behaviors, so those behaviors get them
into trouble.

By finding ways to keep your focus when you need to, you can take control of your ADHD symptoms instead of letting them control you. By developing appropriate outlets, you can be very successful with—or even because of—your ADHD.

IT'S YOUR LIFE!

As much as you may feel stuck in school forever, you really only have a few more years to go. You'll spend most of your life in the adult world, out of school. While you'll probably have a job, you'll also have more freedom to set up your life in a way that works for you. If you hate sitting still, you can find a job that allows you to be active. You have the freedom to choose a career that fits your individual strengths.

Make a list of aspects of a job that are important to you, such as variety, mental stimulation, ability to use your creativity, or making discoveries. Talk with a career counselor who can help you find a realistic career that meets all or most of these needs.

TO BE CONTINUED

Your ADHD symptoms may disappear as you get older, or you may continue to struggle with ADHD into adulthood. Either way, learning to cope with these challenges will help you succeed in all areas of your life, both now and in the future. As you begin to recognize your unique strengths, you will gain the confidence and skill to take control of your ADHD and your life.

ASK YOURSELF THIS

- *What positive labels can you use to describe yourself? How would you explain your strengths to other people? What disadvantages do you see in your life? Are there any ways to turn them into advantages?*

- *If your ADHD were a rocket engine powering you to new heights, where would you want it to take you? What other powerful metaphors can you think of for your ADHD traits?*

- *Who are your heroes—the people you admire most? What are some of the traits about them that you admire?*

- *What would you most want people to admire about you?*

JUST THE FACTS

Symptoms of inattention/distractibility include making careless mistakes, being easily distracted, having trouble focusing, difficulty following through on instructions, disorganization, and losing pencils, books, or assignments.

Symptoms of hyperactivity/impulsivity include fidgeting or squirming, feeling restless, being continually on the go, nonstop talking, interrupting, and blurting out answers before the questions are finished.

People whose close family members have ADHD seem more likely to have it themselves.

According to the US Centers for Disease Control and Prevention (CDC), approximately 5.4 million children from ages 4 to 17 (9.5 percent) were diagnosed with ADHD in 2007.

Also according to the US CDC, boys are more than twice as likely as girls to have ADHD.

Sometimes it's hard for other people to understand who you really are apart from your behavior.

Distractibility can come from problems in the brain's system of filtering out unimportant information.

People who act impulsively often don't think about the consequences of their actions.

People with ADHD symptoms often have grades that swing wildly from high to low, depending on whether their symptoms are flaring up or not.

A little bit of fidgeting, and giving your mind appropriate distractions, can actually help your brain focus.

Scientists think that stimulant medications work by providing internal stimulation to brains that are stimulation starved.

Keeping your blood sugar balanced and exercising regularly are two key components to managing ADHD.

Many brilliant and successful people such as Albert Einstein, Walt Disney, and President John F. Kennedy are believed to have had ADHD symptoms.

WHERE TO TURN

If You Think You Might Have ADHD
Read articles and books by qualified experts such as doctors or brain scientists. Make sure you get evaluated for other potential issues too, such as vision or hearing problems, dyslexia, thyroid issues, anxiety, or depression. Because the evaluation is subjective, be sure to get a second opinion if you are unsure about one doctor's diagnosis.

If You Feel Like No One Understands You
There are many different support groups, both online and in person. Just reading other people's stories is often very helpful because it shows you are not alone, and other people may have come up with great solutions. Search online for "ADHD Support Group" and your city and state, or visit the Children and Adults with Attention-Deficit/Hyperactivity Disorder Web site (www.chadd.org). If you are feeling depressed or suicidal, the National Suicide Hotlines are toll free and staffed 24 hours a day, seven days a week at 1-800-SUICIDE (1-800-784-2433) or 1-800-273-TALK (1-800-273-8255).

If You Have Trouble Managing Your Time
You're not alone. Many millions of people struggle with time management. Fortunately, it's not difficult with the right tools, and there are lots of those. Web sites such as Getting Things Done and ZenHabits feature useful tips.

In addition to David Allen's book *Getting Things Done*, Sean Covey's *The 7 Habits Of Highly Effective Teens*, and Julie Morgenstern's *Organizing from the Inside Out for Teens* are books written especially for teens.

If Your Parents Might Have ADHD

All children need to be able to rely on their parents. Sometimes parents' unmanaged ADHD can pose extra challenges for teens. If your house is too cluttered or chaotic, it may amplify your own ADHD symptoms. If you feel like you can safely talk to your parents, tell them honestly about how their behaviors are affecting you. Tell them what you're learning about your own issues, and suggest that you work on them together. It may end up being a great bonding experience!

Otherwise, talk to someone you trust, such as your doctor or a family friend. Whatever happens, try to carve out a space of your own, free from clutter and chaos, where you can work undisturbed.

GLOSSARY

deficit
A lack or impairment in a functional capacity.

diagnosis
The art or act of identifying a disease from its signs and symptoms.

distractibility
The state or condition of having trouble keeping one's attention on a single thing or person.

dopamine
A chemical in the brain that helps a person experience stimulation.

entrepreneur
One who organizes, manages, and assumes the risk of a business or enterprise.

epidemic
Affecting a disproportionately large number of individuals within a population, community, or region at the same time.

genetics
A branch of biology that deals with the heredity and variation of organisms.

hereditary
Genetically transmitted or transmittable from parent to offspring.

hyperactivity
The state or condition of being excessively or pathologically active.

impulsivity
A tendency to act without thinking of possible consequences.

inattention
Failure to pay attention.

individualized education plan (IEP)
A written plan developed for a child with learning disabilities to accommodate the child's unique learning requirements.

neuron
A cell with specialized processes that is the fundamental functional unit of nervous tissue.

neurotransmitter
A substance that transmits nerve impulses from one neuron to another.

novelty
Something new or unusual.

receptor
A chemical group or molecule on the cell surface or in the cell interior that has an affinity for a specific chemical group, molecule, or virus.

stimulant
A category of drugs that elevate the mood and increase alertness; includes cocaine, methamphetamine, and Ritalin.

stimulate
To excite to activity, growth, or greater activity.

subjective
Arising out of or identified by means of one's perception of one's own states and processes.

ADDITIONAL RESOURCES

SELECTED BIBLIOGRAPHY

Eide, Brock, and Fernette Eide. *The Mislabeled Child*. New York: Hyperion, 2007. Print.

Honos-Webb, Lara. *The Gift of ADHD: How to Transform Your Child's Problems into Strengths*. 2nd ed. Oakland, CA: New Harbinger, 2010. Print.

Klingberg, Torkel. *The Overflowing Brain: Information Overload and the Limits of Working Memory*. New York: Oxford UP, 2009. Print.

Kutscher, Martin. *ADHD: Living Without Brakes*. Philadelphia: Jessica Kingsley, 2008. Print.

FURTHER READINGS

Armstrong, Thomas. *Neurodiversity: Discovering the Extraordinary Gifts of Autism, ADHD, Dyslexia, and Other Brain Differences*. Philadelphia: Perseus, 2010. Print.

Breggin, Peter R. *The Ritalin Fact Book*. Cambridge, MA: Perseus, 2002. Print.

Levine, Mel. *Ready or Not, Here Life Comes!* New York: Simon & Shuster, 2005. Print.

Taylor, Blake E. S. *ADHD & Me: What I Learned From Lighting Fires At the Dinner Table*. Oakland, CA: New Harbinger, 2008. Print.

WEB LINKS

To learn more about living with ADHD, visit ABDO Publishing Company online at **www.abdopublishing.com**. Web sites about living with ADHD are featured on our Book Links page. These links are routinely monitored and updated to provide the most current information available.

SOURCE NOTES

CHAPTER 1. MY LIFE ON FAST FORWARD

1. "What are the symptoms of ADHD in children?" *National Institute of Mental Health*. US National Institute of Mental Health, 23 Jan. 2009. Web. 15 Dec. 2010.

2. "A New Milestone in ADHD History: Dr. Gonzalo Rodriguez-Lafora (1917) and the Unstables." *Atypon*. Atypon Systems Inc., Feb. 2010. Web. 7 Jan. 2011.

3. "Will Smith, Love, Paranoia and the Politics of Booty." *Rolling Stone*. Rolling Stone, n.d. Web. 15 Dec. 2010.

4. Rebecca Winters Keegan. "The Legend of Will Smith." *TIME*. TIME, 29 Nov. 2007. Web. 15 Dec. 2010.

CHAPTER 2. WHY ME? CAUSES AND RISK FACTORS

1. "Heredity as a Cause of ADHD." *myadhd.com*. MyADHD.com, n.d. Web. 26 Dec. 2010.

2. Ibid.

3. "Nearly One Million Children in U.S. Potentially Misdiagnosed With ADHD, Study Finds." *ScienceDaily*. ScienceDaily, 17 Aug. 2010. Web. 15 Dec. 2010.

4. Megan Brooks. "Exposure to smoke, lead ups risk of ADHD." *Reuters*. Thomson Reuters, 24 Nov. 2009. Web. 26 Dec. 2010.

5. Edward Swing, Douglas A. Gentile, Craig A. Anderson, and David A. Walsh. "Television and Video Game Exposure and the Development of Attention Problems." *Pediatrics*. American Academy of Pediatrics, 5 July 2010. Web. 26 Dec. 2010.

6. Ronald D. Chervin, Kristen Hedger Archbold, James E. Dillon, Kenneth J. Pituch, Parviz Panahi, Ronald E. Dahl, and Christian Guilleminault. "SLEEP—Associations Between Symptoms of Inattention, Hyperactivity, Restless Legs, and Periodic Leg Movements." *SLEEP*. Associated Professional Sleep Societies, 15 Mar. 2002. Web. 26 Dec. 2010.

7. Edward Swing, Douglas A. Gentile, Craig A. Anderson, and David A. Walsh. "Television and Video Game Exposure and the Development of Attention Problems." *Pediatrics*. American Academy of Pediatrics, 5 July 2010. Web. 26 Dec. 2010.

8. Torkel Klingberg. *The Overflowing Brain: Information Overload and the Limits of Working Memory*. New York: Oxford UP, 2009. Print. 165–166.

9. Neal Gabler. *Walt Disney: The Triumph of the American Imagination*. New York: Vintage, 2007. 28. Print.

10. "Awards for Walt Disney." *IMDb*. IMDb.com, n.d. Web. 26 Dec. 2010.

CHAPTER 3. AS IF LIFE WEREN'T HARD ENOUGH: COMPLICATIONS

1. "7 Myths about AD/HD…Debunked!" *ADDitude*. New Hope Media, Aug./Sept. 2005. Web. 7 Jan. 2011.

2. Blake E.S. Taylor. *ADHD & Me: What I Learned From Lighting Fires At the Dinner Table*. Oakland, CA: New Harbinger, 2008. Print. 26.

CHAPTER 4. WELL, DO I HAVE IT? TESTS AND DIAGNOSIS

1. "Summary Health Statistics for U.S. Children: National Health Interview Survey, 2006." *Centers for Disease Control and Prevention*. Centers for Disease Control and Prevention, Sept. 2007. Web. 15 Dec. 2010.

2. Ibid.

3. "Diagnosed Attention Deficit Hyperactivity Disorder and Learning Disability: United States, 2004–2006." *Centers for Disease Control and Prevention*. Centers for Disease Control and Prevention, July 2008. Web. 15 Dec. 2010.

SOURCE NOTES CONTINUED

4. Bonnie Cramond. "The Coincidence of Attention Deficit Hyperactivity Disorder and Creativity." *Born to Explore*. National Research Center on the Gifted and Talented, Mar. 1995. Web. 10 Jan. 2011.

CHAPTER 5. GETTING HELP: TREATMENT METHODS

None.

CHAPTER 6. MAKING YOUR LIFE WORK: COPING STRATEGIES

1. Bethany Kochan. "Proper Body Hydration Percentage." *Livestrong.com*. Demand Media, 11 Oct. 2010. Web. 10 Jan. 2011.

2. Dalouge Smith. "The Art of Competitiveness." *Sign On San Diego*. The San Diego Union Tribune, 29 Oct. 2008. Web. 6 Feb. 2011.

CHAPTER 7. STANDING TOGETHER: GIVING AND GETTING SUPPORT

1. Thomas Armstrong. *Neurodiversity: Discovering the Extraordinary Gifts of Autism, ADHD, Dyslexia, and Other Brain Differences*. Philadelphia: Perseus, 2010. Print. 3.

2. Arthur Mitchell. *JFK and his Irish Heritage*. Dublin: Moytura, 1993. Print. 145.

CHAPTER 8. LOVING YOUR ADHD

1. Mel Levine. *Ready or Not, Here Life Comes!* New York: Simon & Shuster, 2005. Print. Back cover.

2. Icon Group International. *Imagination: Webster's Quotations, Facts and Phrases*. San Diego: ICON Group International, 2008. Print. 12.

3. Heidi Reinholdt. *The Quotable Graduate*. Guilford, CT: Globe Pequot, 2003. Print. 110.

4. "ADHD Awareness Day." *ADDA*. Attention Deficit Disorder Association, n.d. Web. 6 Jan. 2011.

5. Ibid.

6. Anne Underwood. "The Gift Of Adhd?" *Newsweek*. The Newsweek/Daily Beast Company, 14 Mar. 2005. Web. 27 Jan. 2011.

7. Deborah Hedstrom-Page. *From Telegraph to Light Bulb with Thomas Edison*. Nashville, TN: B&H, 2007. Print. 76.

INDEX

ABOUT THE AUTHOR

Tad Kershner's writing has appeared in several magazines, and he has won awards for screenwriting and short fiction. Kershner was a youth-group leader for several years. He lives in the Pacific Northwest with his wife and teenage son and enjoys going on kayaking, hiking, and biking adventures with his family and friends. He holds a degree in filmmaking and was once a professional video editor.

PHOTO CREDITS

Charles Benavidez/iStockphoto, cover, 1; Otna Ydur/ Bigstock, 8; Hongqi Zhang/Bigstock, 10, 54; Chris Vaughan/ Bigstock, 16; Mark & Audrey Gibson/Photolibrary, 18; Losevsky Pavel/Shutterstock Images, 25; iStockphoto, 28, 40; Elena Elisseeva/Bigstock, 31; Wavebreak Media Ltd/ Bigstock, 34; Cathy Yeulet/Bigstock, 37, 48; Lisa F. Young/ Bigstock, 45, 80; Michal Bednarek/Shutterstock Images, 51; Konstantin Yolshin/Shutterstock Images, 58; Testing/ Shutterstock Images, 62; David Davis/Bigstock, 67; Suprijono Suharjoto/Bigstock, 72; Kharidehal Abhirama Ashwin/ Shutterstock Images, 74; Tracy Whiteside/Bigstock, 76; Edhar Yuualaits/Bigstock, 84; Dmitriy Shironosov/Bigstock, 86; Hill Street Studios/Photolibrary, 91; Sorin Alb/Shutterstock Images, 93; Andres Rodriguez/Bigstock, 95